Raging Rocky

Written By: Syreeta Washington
Illustrated By: J. W. McVeigh

Afterword Provided By:
Dr. Tamiko Smith, School Psychologist

Copyright © 2016 Syreeta Washington.

All rights reserved.

www.Butterflybooks.us

ISBN: 0997982004

ISBN-13: 978-0997982008

Library of Congress Control Number: 2016914498
Butterfly Books, Ewing, NJ

Illustrations by JW McVeigh

No part of this publication may be reproduced, distributed, or transmitted in any form or by any means, including photocopying, recording, or other electronic or mechanical methods, without the prior written permission of the publisher, except in the case of brief quotations embodied in critical reviews and certain other noncommercial uses permitted by copyright law.

For permission requests, send an email to the publisher, addressed "Attention: Permissions Coordinator."

Ordering Information:
Quantity sales. Special discounts are available on quantity purchases by educational institutions, non-profits, corporations, associations, and others.

For details, visit www.butterflybooks.us.

Printed in the United States of America

DEDICATION
Dedicated to my sister - my first playmate, student and best friend.

I'm a good student
and I think school is okay
But my favorite part of the day
is when I go outside
to play!

When I'm outside
I get to do
all kinds of things
like play
hide and seek

My favorite thing to do
is to play any sport!

You can find me in the
playground
on the basketball court.

When I play a game,
I love to be on the winning team.

We always cheer and shout and make a big scene!

But when I'm on the losing team
it makes me feel sad.
I worked so hard to win
that I start to get mad.

Sometimes when I get mad,
I yell and I shout.
I feel so upset
I have to let it all out!

Whenever we lose a game
I don't like it one bit.
I jump up and down,
throwing a fit!
I feel so upset that I
want to shove and hit!

My coach and my dad
tell me to be a good sport
and that win or lose
we are all friends on the court.

But when we lose a game, I feel sad and mean. I feel so angry that I can't play on their team.

One day, after we lost a game
I got **so, so** mad!
I kicked the ball <u>*high*</u> into the trees
and it was the only one that we had.

Right away I felt sorry,
I didn't *mean* to kick the ball away.
I just got *so* upset
that we lost the game that day.

I stomped over to the bench
feeling upset and wearing a frown.
I wanted to do my best
to try to calm down.

But all my bad feelings
bubbled up from inside,
on top of each other
they started to crash and collide.

Later, after the other kids all went home
I sat on the bench feeling all alone.

My coach sat next to me,
and tapped my shoulder to say,
"Rocky, what happened
to make you act that way?"

I slumped my shoulders and explained to him
that I can't stand to lose, it's important to win!

I told him that when I lose
I start to feel so mad,
it builds up inside
and makes me act bad.

My coach said,
"Rocky, you are really good on the court.
I can teach you not to be
such a poor sport.
When I was a cub, I was just like you.
I couldn't stand to lose,
so I would blow up too."

I lifted my head
and looked him in the eye
surprised because my coach
seems like such a nice guy.
I knew
if he could beat anger
so could I.

So, that day we started
to talk it all out.
I told him that anger
makes me scream and shout!

He asked me if I could draw anger
what it would be
and I drew a picture
of a big storm inside of me.

My coach nodded and said,
"When I was a cub
I would get mad and pout.
Yes, anger can feel
like a storm swirling about."

"It can turn faster and faster
spinning out of control
which is why
learning to calm down
is our final goal."

He said, "I want you to imagine the feelings
swirling and turning around.
Then imagine them slowly falling to the
ground. One by one
all the angry feelings drifting along
like snowflakes melting
in the middle of your palm.

As each one begins to melt away
remember how much fun it is to play.
Yes, it feels bad when you don't win
but there's always a chance to play again."

After that day,
when I played with my friends
I still felt a little mad when I didn't win.

And whenever bad feelings started to race,
I used my new tools to put anger in its place.
I remembered my coach's words
to use as my guide
to control the snow storm of feelings inside.

ACKNOWLEDGEMENTS
Special thanks to Dorra J. who helped make this possible!

ABOUT THE AUTHOR

Syreeta Washington is an experienced motivational speaker and life coach. She conceived of the "I'm Cool" book series as a way to normalize typical childhood behavior but also to highlight the awesomeness inside of all children. She is very proud of the first book in the series, Jumping Jack. Syreeta is also a full-time psychology professor who is passionate about engaging her students in challenging and fun ways in her courses.

She while a Philly native, she currently resides in New Jersey with her quirky family, precocious cat and fantabulous dog whose antics light up her days.

ABOUT THE ILLUSTRATOR

Jonathan W. McVeigh is a high school chemistry teacher that has a background in chemical engineering. He possesses a BS in chemical Engineering and a MA in Curriculum, Instruction, and Supervision. After finding a major passion of his was in education, Jonathan converted from engineering to teaching. Always enjoying the arts from when he was very little, Jonathan grew up drawing superheroes, cartoons, and monsters. With his experience in the classroom and personal connections to learning challenges, he seeks to use his talents to inspire students to believe in themselves. When given the opportunity to use his artistic hobby to further aid students, he partnered with Syreeta Washington to help make the "I'm Cool" Book Series. Currently, he is employed as a high school chemistry teacher and is a part-time professor in chemistry and physics at a local college.

He currently resides in NJ and really likes Reese's Peanut Butter Cups.

AFTERWORD

The following contribution was generously provided by Dr. Tamiko Smith, Clinical Director & School Psychologist. We are very grateful for her input and feel it will be of value to you.

It is normal to feel angry. It's a human emotion that we all have. The point of this story is to normalize anger and provide a vehicle for discussing its management. Anger is a "normal emotion with a wide range of intensity from mild irritation and frustration to rage." It becomes of concern when children have extreme difficulty in controlling their anger and the behaviors escalate to the "point of being out of control." This is exhibited by extended periods of temper outbursts, blackouts, rage, hitting, kicking, biting and other physically and verbally aggressive behavior. Mismanaged anger can be counterproductive and unhealthy.

Anger has three components:
1. Physical reactions (physiological responses and "fight or flight responses")
2. Cognitive experiences (how we perceive and think about what is making us angry) and
3. Behavior (the way we express our anger)

The primary goal of "Raging Rocky" is to provide children, parents, schools and clinicians with a tool to help facilitate the discussion about understanding anger and to help children develop positive coping skills to manage their "bouts of uncontrollable anger."

When children can manage anger in a positive way it allows for personal growth, improved peer relationships and better decision making.

Questions for Discussion, Counseling and Academic Lesson Planning

- ⇒ In the story, why does Rocky get upset?
- ⇒ What does Rocky do when he is mad?
- ⇒ How does it make his friends feel when he acts that way?
- ⇒ How do you feel when you lose a game?
- ⇒ What does Rocky learn how to do when he gets angry?
- ⇒ Who helps Rocky when he gets mad? Who can help you when you get mad?
- ⇒ Draw a picture of what your anger looks like when you are upset.
- ⇒ Name 3 things (to the reader: you can replace this with the term "tools" and discuss how tools are designed to help us) you can do that would help you manage your anger when you get upset?

Keep a copy of these 3 things (tools) in your backpack or in your pocket. They will help you with your anger while playing with your friends at school and home.

www.ingramcontent.com/pod-product-compliance
Lightning Source LLC
LaVergne TN
LVHW072058070426
835508LV00002B/161